Rachel Cruze Presents:

THE GRADUATE'S SURVIVAL GUIDE

Setting you up for Success in College

YOUR MONEY
ANSWERS TO COMMON QUESTIONS

D0053121

This publication is designed to provide accurate and authoritative information with regard to the subject matter covered. It is sold with the understanding that the publisher is not engaged in rendering financial, accounting or other professional advice. If financial advice or other expert assistance is required, the services of a competent professional should be sought.

Editorial: Christy Wright, Michelle Grooms, Darcie Clemen and Robert Bruce

Cover Design: Brian Williams

Interior Design: Scott Lee Designs {scottleedesigns.com}

ISBN: 978-1-937077-00-6

TABLE OF CONTENTS

ABOUT RACHEL CRUZE

Growing up as a Ramsey kid, Rachel learned the basic principles of money at an early age. Dave and Sharon Ramsey taught her how to save, spend, and give—valuable lessons she uses in everyday life.

Today, she's passing on those principles to others in her generation. Rachel is an experienced communicator who has been speaking to audiences as large as 10,000 people since she was 15. Since joining Dave's team full time in 2010, she has traveled the country speaking about the dangers of credit cards and debt at high schools, colleges and youth conferences. She shows teens and young adults how to budget their money, intentionally save for things like cars and college, and give.

Rachel has a B.A. in Communication Studies from the University of Tennessee. She lives with her husband, Winston, in Franklin, Tennessee.

INTRODUCTION FROM RACHEL CRUZE

So many college students have basic questions about money. Why should you start saving? How do you make a budget? When should you think about buying a car? When should you start investing? It can all be overwhelming.

That's what this book is for. For years, people have told my dad, Dave Ramsey, that they wish they had learned how to manage money before college. *The Graduate's Survival Guide* covers the basics— from saving and budgeting to finding jobs and making big purchases— everything future college students need to know before they set foot on a college campus.

If you can grasp this stuff now as a graduating senior and learn from the financial mistakes others have made, you will be a step ahead of most students. You'll be well on your way to being in control of your money throughout school.

I'm passionate about this material. I want to take the lessons my dad taught me and pass them on to my generation—high school students, college students, even young adults. If you stay out of debt, live on a plan, save, and start investing, you will become wealthy one day.

Use this book as a resource to help you through school. While reading it, think about everything you can do and everyone you can help if you have a debt-free college experience and graduate with a pile of cash in the bank. This material can literally change your life!

"YOU WILL EITHER LEARN HOW TO MANAGE MONEY OR THE LACK OF IT WILL ALWAYS MANAGE YOU." — DAVE RAMSEY

THE GRADUATE'S SURVIVAL GUIDE

Setting you Up For Success in College

HOW DO I KNOW IF I SHOULD GO TO COLLEGE?

Answer

FIRST, THINK ABOUT WHETHER OR NOT A DEGREE IN YOUR CHOSEN FIELD WILL ACTUALLY OPEN UP CAREER OPPORTUNITIES. The truth is that, in many fields, a degree won't open doors for you. Consider whether the cost of the diploma will bring you a financial return in the long run. Is that General Studies degree worth the amount of money you will be paying for it?

Second, you should go to college if you believe that your quality of life will improve. Maybe you think college will be a good personal growth experience for you, or maybe you're thinking God is leading you down that path. No matter what your reason, remember to go slow and pay cash. You'll avoid getting into financial trouble down the road.

If you do decide to go to college, don't make your future hostage to student loans. Make wise choices based on the amount of money you currently have, plus your income while you are attending school—assuming you'll be working.

Remember, college is extremely important, but you have to make smart financial decisions before you go to school—or else you're going to pay the consequences when you get out.

I'M 18 YEARS OLD AND I WAS HOMESCHOOLED. MY DAD WORKS FOR A COLLEGE CLOSE TO HOME, SO I COULD ATTEND THERE FOR FREE. I'M ALSO LOOKING AT ANOTHER SCHOOL MORE GEARED TOWARD WHAT I WANT TO DO, BUT IT WILL COST ME A LOT MORE MONEY AND IT'S FARTHER AWAY. HOWEVER, IT'S A CHRISTIAN SCHOOL AND THAT APPEALS TO ME TOO. I'M NOT SURE WHAT TO DO.

Answer

IF YOU CAN AFFORD TO GO TO THE MORE EXPENSIVE SCHOOL, MEANING NO STUDENT LOANS, THEN GO FOR IT. If that school has something you are passionate about doing, and you don't mind being farther away from home, then it could be a great experience for you. Just don't go into debt for it. That's a bad plan from the start.

Keep this in mind, though: Christian colleges provide some great spiritual support, but don't be under any illusion that a Christian school is perfect just because it says "Christian" in the brochure. Some of the characters you'll meet on any Christian campus are just as wild and crazy as some you'd see facedown on the quad at a state school!

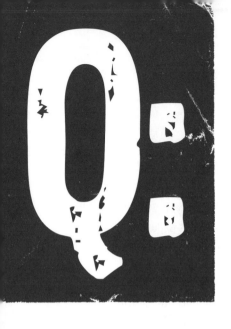

I ONLY HAVE ENOUGH MONEY TO ATTEND A JUNIOR COLLEGE. WILL THIS AFFECT MY ABILITY TO BE HIRED?

Answer

If the junior college has quality teachers and classes, and you work hard and learn, then **ALL YOU'LL NEED IS AN OPPORTUNITY TO PROVE YOURSELF.**

Some major, multizillion-dollar corporations will look down on junior colleges, and it may affect you in certain areas. But think about this: 98% of American companies have fewer than 100 employees. That means most employers have small teams; therefore, they're more likely to get to know you during the interview process and not just look at which college is listed on your resume.

Our company has about 300 team members, and not one of those people was hired based on where they went to school or even on what their GPA was. There are a thousand more important things to look at, such as character, poise, excellence in a particular field, experience and the drive to get things done. These are the things that make great team members.

If you're still skittish about a junior college, then spend time researching your in-state options at state schools. Residents usually get a fantastic deal on in-state tuition. And of course, you should make scholarship hunting your new part-time job for a while!

> **"THERE ARE DREAMERS AND THERE ARE PLANNERS; THE PLANNERS MAKE THEIR DREAMS COME TRUE."** — EDWIN LOUIS COLE

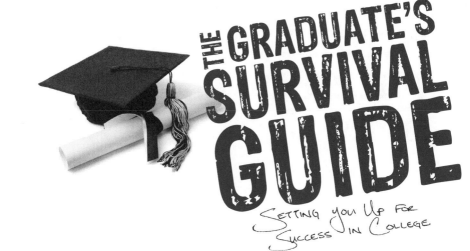

THE GRADUATE'S SURVIVAL GUIDE

Setting you Up for Success in College

MY PARENTS WILL BE PAYING FOR EVERYTHING WHILE I'M IN COLLEGE. WHY DO I NEED TO LEARN HOW TO MANAGE MONEY?

Answer

DID YOU KNOW THAT 70% OF AMERICANS LIVE PAYCHECK TO PAYCHECK? That means they spend everything they make and they're broke again until the next payday. They are one emergency away from financial disaster.

Why do they live this way? Many never learned how to manage their money. They developed poor financial habits and either don't know how or don't care enough to correct them. By learning how to manage money now, you'll avoid the money mistakes most people make. And it's easier to learn good financial habits than it is to change bad ones.

In just a few years you'll be out of school and on your own too. College is your chance to build character and become a mature, successful adult. Too many people party through college and put off growing up until they find themselves on their own with a family depending on them to survive. But they never established good personal habits or learned the skills they need to succeed.

Learning how to manage money now is your first step toward changing that cycle.

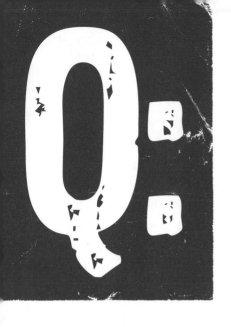

HOW SHOULD I PREPARE TO MANAGE MY MONEY WHEN I GO OFF TO COLLEGE, AND WHAT SHOULD I DO WHEN I'M THERE?

Answer

FIRST OFF, WITHOUT A DOUBT, AVOID CREDIT CARDS. They will tempt you on every corner. You need to learn how to operate, balance, and reconcile a checking account. You also need to learn how to do a zero-based budget. That just means you'll do a budget every month, planning ahead what you're going to do with every dollar you get. You write your income at the top, then write every expense down under it, including savings and giving. Subtract all the expenses from the income, and it should equal zero.

So, if you get $100 a month from your parents, and you make $400 a month at your job, then you need to write out a written plan for that $500 every single month, before the month begins. Categorize your entertainment budget, your food budget, your bills—everything you spend on a monthly basis. Tell every dollar where to go. That way, you don't have any loose dollars running around and you maintain control over your money.

I'VE MADE THE CHOICE TO WORK MY WAY THROUGH COLLEGE SO I WON'T GRADUATE WITH STUDENT LOAN DEBT. I'VE ALSO GOT A PLAN TO SAVE UP AN EMERGENCY FUND WHILE I'M WORKING AND GOING TO SCHOOL. BUT I KNOW I'LL NEED A BETTER CAR BY THE TIME I GRADUATE COLLEGE, AND I WANT TO START INVESTING AND PLANNING FOR MY FUTURE FAMILY. HOW DO YOU PRIORITIZE AND MANAGE SAVING FOR ALL THESE THINGS WITHOUT FEELING OVERWHELMED?

Answer

Congratulations on your commitment to stay out of debt! You're already making decisions that will put you in a great position once you graduate.

Thinking about the future can be overwhelming. **THE GOOD NEWS IS YOU DON'T HAVE TO DO EVERYTHING RIGHT NOW.** You've got a great plan for this point in your life. There's no doubt you'll be able to make plans to reach the other goals you mentioned. But right now, getting through college is your number-one priority.

After that, you can take a look at the other stuff. You have plenty of time to decide what's important to you and plan for it when the time comes. You've got years to figure it out! So don't feel overwhelmed. Things are much easier to deal with when you break them down into small steps. No one can do four things at once and still manage to do them well.

Just decide what matters most and put it at the top of your list. Put everything else in descending order of importance. Then go down the list and knock them out one at a time.

WHY SHOULD I MANUALLY BALANCE MY ACCOUNT WHEN I CHECK MY ONLINE BALANCE DAILY?

Answer

YOU HAVE PROBABLY WRITTEN CHECKS OR USED YOUR DEBIT CARD FOR SOMETHING THAT HASN'T CLEARED THE BANK YET. Those are called outstanding checks or outstanding debit card charges. If you withdraw money based on your online balance, and one of those outstanding items clears while there is not much money in your account, you'll have an overdraft—along with a hefty fee.

So keep your account balanced. Most banks make this easier than ever nowadays by giving you access to all your account information online. If you take advantage of that, and especially if you use budget software or online tools, it should only take you a few minutes a week to keep everything up to date. At the very least, you need to do this once a month.

Bottom line: The bank doesn't know if you've written a check that hasn't been cashed yet, and they don't know if you swiped your debit card at a store that takes a day or two to process charges. Don't take the chance. You—and only you—are responsible for making sure your account stays balanced!

SINCE I'M A STUDENT WITH NO MONEY, NO ASSETS AND NO CREDIT HISTORY, DO I NEED TO WORRY ABOUT PROTECTING MY IDENTITY?

YOU ARE NEVER TOO YOUNG TO BE CAREFUL WITH YOUR PERSONAL INFORMATION. Even dogs have been known to get credit card offers, so you can't trust credit card companies or other lending institutions to be thorough about checking their credit applicants.

You can protect yourself from identity theft by taking these steps:

- Use a paper shredder to destroy all credit card offers and bank statements.

- Remove your Social Security number and driver's license number from your checks.

- Write "Photo ID Required" in the signature space of your debit card.

- Create strong passwords using a combination of letters, characters and numbers.

- Keep passwords and personal information confidential.

You should also check your credit report from the three credit bureaus at least once a year. You can get a free copy of your report at annualcreditreport.com. Immediately alert the credit bureau of any errors you find.

You can also get good identity theft protection insurance dirt cheap.

It's one of the types of insurance we recommend everyone get. Just be careful; there are a lot of worthless ID theft services out there. Make sure you only buy a plan that includes restoration services. That means someone else will clean up the mess if your identity gets stolen.

YOU ARE NEVER TOO YOUNG TO BE CAREFUL WITH YOUR PERSONAL INFORMATION.

PEOPLE AGES 18–29 ARE THE NUMBER-ONE TARGET OF IDENTITY THIEVES.

QUEST COMMUNICATIONS

Q:

I WAS WONDERING WHY I NEED HEALTH INSURANCE WHILE I'M IN COLLEGE. I'M A HEALTHY GUY.

Answer

Accidents happen. You can be walking to class and step off the curb and twist your ankle. **HEALTHY COLLEGE STUDENTS GET SICK.** It happens all the time. When those types of things happen, you need health insurance.

One of the leading causes of bankruptcy in America today is financial problems due to a lack of health insurance. Your best option is to get on your parents' policy if they have one. It won't cost them much to add you and keep you in the family plan. If you're still in college, you should qualify for that.

Even if you buy your own policy, it shouldn't cost you that much at your age. If you don't have health insurance, you're taking one of the biggest financial risks you can possibly take.

I AM REALLY STRUGGLING WITH THE IDEA OF NOT BUILDING MY CREDIT SCORE. EVERYONE SAYS I NEED IT. HOW CAN I PROVE THAT I AM GOOD AT HANDLING MY MONEY WITHOUT IT?

Answer

THE WAY TO PROVE YOU ARE GOOD AT HANDLING MONEY IS BY HAVING MONEY. A stupid little number on a credit report doesn't do that.

Here's a test: Is there any money in your bank account? That's how you tell if you have money. Your net worth (what you own minus what you owe), your income and your cash on hand is your test score for whether you're winning with money, not some stupid credit score.

The FICO score is an "I love debt score." You know how it is calculated? It is 100% based on debt—how much you owe, how often you make payments, how often you borrow, etc. This dumb number simply shows that you are good at borrowing money. It has absolutely nothing to do with how much you make or how much you have in the bank. It's even possible to be a multibillionaire and still have a horrible credit score. How does that make sense?

Millionaires tell us that the number-one way to be successful with money is to remain debt free. So, you can be broke and miserable with a fantastic credit score, or you could be a carefree millionaire with no credit score. Which sounds better to you?

FICO stands for Fair Isaac Corporation, which developed a score-based rating system that many companies use to measure an individual's credit risk. Although this measurement has become widely accepted, it is a faulty standard that is based on debt, not wealth.

FIVE COMPONENTS OF THE FICO SCORE

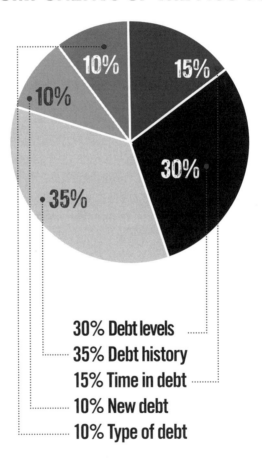

30% Debt levels
35% Debt history
15% Time in debt
10% New debt
10% Type of debt

23% OF TEENS KNOW WHAT A CREDIT SCORE IS.

CHARLES SCHWAB SURVEY

> **"THE RICH RULES OVER THE POOR, AND THE BORROWER IS THE SLAVE OF THE LENDER."**
> — PROVERBS 22:7 NRSV

THE GRADUATE'S SURVIVAL GUIDE

Setting you Up for Success in College

IS IT EVER OKAY TO GO INTO DEBT FOR AN EDUCATION?

No. But that doesn't mean you can't get an education. **THERE ALL SORTS OF WAYS TO GET AN EDUCATION AND ACCOMPLISH YOUR GOALS.** It's interesting that a lot of people go into debt not because they want to simply go to college, but because they want to go to a certain type of college.

Don't get caught up in school names and campus lifestyles. If you don't have any money for college, you can go to a two-year community college, work part time, apply for scholarships, and eventually transfer to a state university.

This isn't difficult, but a lot of students and parents don't consider this option because they have their hearts set on a particular school. If you can afford the tuition for your dream school, go for it. But if you can't, you can still get a high-quality, _affordable_ education.

HOW DO I PAY FOR COLLEGE WITHOUT STUDENT LOANS?

Answer

Most people believe you can't be a student without a loan. But it is possible to get through college without going into debt. Here are a few ways you can do it:

- **APPLY FOR SCHOLARSHIPS.** There are tons of small, little-known scholarships out there. If you only get $1,500, that's $1,500 less to come up with on your own.

- **GET A PART-TIME JOB.** This is great for two reasons. First, you'll earn money to help pay for school. Second, the more time you spend working, the less time you have to spend money!

- **WORK FULL TIME IN THE SUMMER.** If you aren't taking summer classes, get a full-time job and save, save, save!

- **BE A RESIDENTIAL ASSISTANT.** These gigs usually have good perks. In exchange for watching over the dorm, you get a paycheck, room and board discounts, parking permits and other goodies.

These are just suggestions. I bet you can think of more things you can do to lighten the money load. It will be a lot of work, but it's worth it if you can graduate without debt. All your broke friends will start looking at you differently. Their comments will eventually change from "Man, you're weird!" to "Man, you're a genius!"

I'M A COLLEGE STUDENT, AND I HAVE THE OPPORTUNITY TO STUDY ABROAD. I DON'T HAVE ANY CAR PAYMENTS, AND I'M PAYING FOR MY TUITION WITHOUT LOANS. STUDYING ABROAD WOULD COST ABOUT $9,000 IN LOANS. SHOULD I DO IT?

ANSWER

Let's pretend you have $10,000 extra in the bank, and you don't need that money for school. If the question was to study abroad or open a Roth IRA, then it would make sense to study abroad, because you've got the cash. But **YOU SHOULDN'T GO INTO DEBT FOR EITHER ONE.**

Studying abroad can be a good thing. More and more students are doing that these days. It's a great opportunity to learn about the world and yourself at the same time. But the payback, certainly in the next decade of your life, does not justify the cost. A better option might be to do some graduate work in a work-study program after you're out of college and in the workforce.

I'M PLANNING TO GET A CREDIT CARD AND USE IT TO PAY BILLS WHILE I'M IN SCHOOL. I'M LOOKING FOR A CARD THAT HAS NO ANNUAL FEE AND GIVES ME MONEY BACK ON MY PURCHASES. I'LL PAY THE BALANCE OFF EVERY MONTH. WON'T I COME OUT AHEAD?

Answer

WE SEE PEOPLE EVERY DAY WHO THOUGHT THEY COULD BEAT THE CREDIT CARD COMPANIES AT THEIR OWN GAME. And, in almost every case, using credit cards has come back to bite them.

When you get that credit card, you start the engine of a multibillion-dollar industry that's designed to accomplish one thing—separate you from your money. And they are really good at it! These companies are happy to give you a tiny percentage back, but they're not doing it from the goodness of their hearts. They know, at some point, you'll stumble.

And even if you're the one person out of a hundred who won't get caught in some kind of weird goof or scam, you'll still overspend. People who pay with plastic spend up to 40% more than those who pay with cash!

No millionaire will tell you that credit card rebates made them rich. In fact, most will say that getting out and staying out of debt is the key to building wealth.

The bottom line about credit cards? If you don't play with snakes, you won't get bitten.

"THERE ARE NO SHORTCUTS TO ANY PLACE WORTH GOING." — BEVERLY SILLS

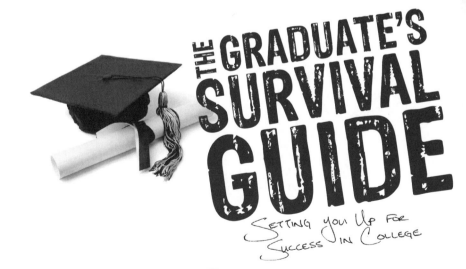

THE GRADUATE'S SURVIVAL GUIDE

SETTING you Up FOR SUCCESS IN COLLEGE

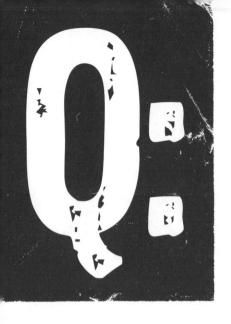

SHOULD I TAKE ADVANTAGE OF 0% INTEREST?

Answer

NO! **ABSOLUTELY NOT!** YOU DON'T WANT TO "TAKE ADVANTAGE" OF 0%. Asking that question is already an indicator that you can't afford whatever it is that you want to buy. You've got the fever, and you figure 0% interest is the way to go. No!

Watch out for the fever. That's when there's sweat on your upper lip and on the palms of your hands. Your eyes dilate. Your protein and endorphin release goes up in your body and, in general, you feel like you NEED some stuff. Stay away from that.

You don't take advantage of 0% interest—it takes advantage of you. Studies show that 88% of the people who take out 90-days-same-as-cash don't pay it off in 90 days. That means they'll be back-charged through the whole contract at the ridiculous rip-off finance company rate—something around 30% or so.

That's basically kicking you in the tail for being so dumb and buying something you really couldn't afford. How do you know if you can afford something? If you can pay for it with cash, you can afford it.

WHAT'S WRONG WITH BUYING THINGS 12-MONTHS-SAME-AS-CASH?

Answer

"SAME AS CASH" IS NOT THE SAME AS CASH. You know what's the same as cash? Cash—and maybe a debit card.

Those 12-months-same-as-cash commercials are all about getting you to buy stuff you can't afford. They make it look easy, but there are always problems. If you'll save up and pay actual cash instead of taking the bait on one of those "deals," you'll avoid a mess that can take months or years to clear up.

That's what happened to one of our clients. She took the 12-months-same-as-cash "deal" and made her payments on time, but the company recorded one of those payments as late. And one late payment means they can charge you 24–38% interest on the whole deal, going all the way back to the day you bought that thing you just couldn't live without.

Even if you're responsible in keeping up with every payment, you're trusting that the credit company won't do something shady to mess you up. Good luck with that. You can avoid the trouble and get a better deal if you pay with cash.

The bottom line: There is no good shortcut for getting the things you want. Save up and pay with cash every time.

I AM GETTING READY TO BUY A NEW LAPTOP, AND I CAN SAVE 15% IF I OPEN A CREDIT CARD ACCOUNT AT THIS LOCAL STORE. WHAT'S WRONG WITH SAVING SOME MONEY IF I CLOSE THE ACCOUNT AFTERWARD?

Answer

First, you will hurt your credit score. **SAVING MONEY AND BUILDING WEALTH MATTERS A LOT MORE THAN CREDIT SCORES.** But you should know that opening an account and turning right back around and closing that account will ding your score.

The biggest problem is that if you play with snakes, you will get bitten. Don't sign up for some 90-days-same-as-cash deal at the register. You're talking about saving the equivalent of a couple of Happy Meals. And in return, you run the risk of getting harassed by credit card companies. That's not a good trade-off.

When you play with these companies, something will get messed up. Your perfect little plan will not work out. When you pay cash 100% of the time, you'll have no repercussions later. You're done. You own it. You walk out of the store without problems later. It's that simple.

"PERSONAL RELATIONSHIPS ARE
THE FERTILE SOIL FROM WHICH ALL
ADVANCEMENT, ALL SUCCESS, ALL
ACHIEVEMENT IN REAL LIFE GROWS."
– BEN STEIN

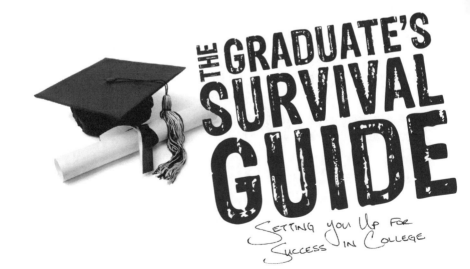

THE GRADUATE'S
SURVIVAL
GUIDE

*Setting you Up For
Success in College*

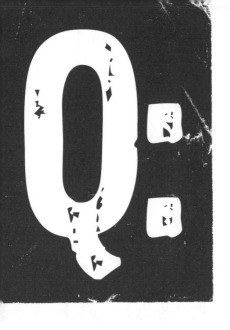

MY OLDER SISTER MAXED OUT HER CREDIT CARDS, AND NOW SHE CAN'T MAKE THE PAYMENTS. THE CREDIT CARD COMPANY IS CALLING MY PARENTS FOUR OR FIVE TIMES A DAY DEMANDING THEM TO PAY THE BILL. WHAT CAN THEY DO?

Your mom and dad need to realize that **THIS COMPANY IS BREAKING FEDERAL LAW.** Your parents are not responsible for your sister's debt—unless they co-signed for the credit cards. The company isn't even allowed to discuss her debt with them.

Your parents need to get an answering machine that will allow them to record phone conversations. The next time this company calls, your parents need to tell the collector that the call is being recorded and that they are not liable for your sister's debt. They should also make sure this company knows they will get sued if they call about your sister's debt again.

Their tactics are in violation of the Federal Fair Debt Collection Practices Act. What they're doing is illegal, immoral and just mean. They're trying to bully your parents into paying this debt, and you can't get rid of a bully by being nice.

If the collectors keep calling after your parents have told them all this, there's another tool we like to use that is particularly effective. It's called an air horn. Give the collector a warning, and then let the air horn wail into the phone. After a few blasts, the collectors should get the message.

MY BOYFRIEND'S CREDIT IS IN BAD SHAPE, AND WE'RE THINKING ABOUT GETTING MARRIED. WILL HIS BAD CREDIT RATING AFFECT MINE? MY CREDIT IS IN GOOD SHAPE RIGHT NOW. I HAVE NO CREDIT CARDS AND MY CAR IS PAID FOR.

Answer

MARRYING SOMEONE WITH A BAD CREDIT RATING WILL NOT AFFECT YOUR SCORE. In other words, the black marks on his credit rating don't jump across the aisle onto your report as soon as he slips the ring on your finger.

Two things will happen after you're married. First, your credit bureau will begin to reflect the fact that he is your husband. He'll be listed as "spouse" on your report. After this, if they pull your report for any reason, they'll see that half of your "team" has had problems in the past.

His credit score could affect you both the most when you decide to buy a home. If he still has credit issues, purchasing a house could be difficult.

But the big issue here is that you seem to have differing views on money management. Make sure you go through premarital counseling together and that the counseling includes a financial component. You could also practice by sitting down together and making a monthly budget. Just keep in mind that this is practice only. Never actually mix your money until your wedding day!

If you get married, then money will be a big part of your relationship for the rest of your lives. Money fights and money problems are the leading cause of divorce, so if you agree on your goals now, you'll set a solid foundation for a healthy marriage.

MY PARENTS PAY FOR MY EDUCATION, CLOTHES, FOOD, TRIPS—BASICALLY EVERYTHING. BUT A LOT OF MY FRIENDS ARE INDEPENDENT FROM THEIR PARENTS. WHEN SHOULD I START PAYING FOR THINGS ON MY OWN? IS THERE ANYTHING WRONG WITH THEM HELPING ME OUT FOR THE NEXT 5–10 YEARS?

Answer

If your parents have done a good job of saving money, there's nothing wrong with them paying for you to go to school and paying for your life while you're in school. That's a goal for a lot of parents, and it's great that your parents have been able to do that.

But **ONCE YOU GRADUATE, IT'S TIME TO GET OUT THERE ON YOUR OWN.** So five to 10 years of your parents paying for your adult life? No way. Not unless you want to be "that guy" who lives in his mother's basement forever. Does that sound fun to you?

Part of being an adult is paying your own bills and making your own way. It's fine for your parents to help until you graduate and maybe for a month or two after that. But once you get that first job, it's time to move on.

"NOTHING WILL WORK UNLESS YOU DO."
— JOHN WOODEN

THE GRADUATE'S SURVIVAL GUIDE

Setting you Up For Success in College

Q.

MY SISTER AND I BOTH GET PAID FOR DOING JOBS AROUND THE HOUSE. IF WE DO ALL OUR JOBS, WE MAKE $50 A WEEK. BUT, IF WE FORGET ONE OR TWO OF THEM, WE GET LESS. DO YOU THINK THIS IS FAIR?

Answer

THAT'S VERY FAIR. Your parents have put you on a commission system instead of just handing you money, and that's a great way to learn how to manage your income.

Money comes from work, period. In the real world, if you don't work, then you don't eat. You also won't have money to do other fun stuff like go to the movies or buy clothes. The value of hard work and doing a job well are important lessons that all kids should learn. Not only that, but all parents should teach this to their children.

Think about how you feel when you get all your work done compared to the times when you don't. Work is rewarding financially and spiritually. But the rewards won't be as great if you don't get the job done!

WORKING

WHAT ARE SOME GOOD STARTING JOBS FOR A TEENAGER WITHOUT MUCH EXPERIENCE?

ANSWER

THERE ARE TWO WAYS TO LOOK AT YOUR WORKING CAREER AS A TEENAGER.

First, you can do it simply for money. This might not be a job that will carry you where you want to go the rest of your life, but you will learn to work and you will be able to meet some of your goals, like buying a car or paying your insurance.

This type of job doesn't have to be something real complicated. Maybe it's cutting grass, babysitting, doing home repairs, bagging groceries, waiting tables, or some other type of manual labor. These types of jobs will teach you how to be responsible and follow through on your commitments.

Your other option is to take a job that doesn't really pay you very much (it may pay you nothing) but allows you to hang around and participate in a career field that you may want to work in one day.

You probably won't be doing anything except making copies and getting people coffee, but you'll get to learn the business by watching all of the insiders. You may not be paid anything, or maybe just a small amount, but this type of job is more about the experience anyway.

WHAT CAN YOU PUT ON A PART-TIME JOB APPLICATION THAT WILL MAKE YOU STAND OUT FROM EVERYONE ELSE?

ANSWER

WELL, EXPERIENCE IS THE OBVIOUS ANSWER. It's a great thing to have when you're looking for work. Every employer wants to know that a potential employee can do the job.

But even if it's your first "real" job, you probably have experience you might not realize. If you've ever done babysitting, that's experience. It's even better if the parents will give you a good recommendation. If they feel comfortable with you caring for their child, then chances are a fast-food manager can trust you to flip a few burgers.

While you're in school, hold a seat on the student council, play sports, or do some other extracurricular activity. These things will catch a manager's eye. They all show that you're willing to work, commit to something, and take on responsibility.

HOW SHOULD YOU DRESS FOR A PART-TIME JOB INTERVIEW?

Answer

Whether a job is part-time or full-time, you should **DRESS IN A MANNER THAT'S APPROPRIATE**. This doesn't always mean a suit and tie, but it doesn't mean jeans and a concert T-shirt either.

The way you dress for an interview says something about your level of maturity. Some managers even take it as an indication of respect (or a lack of respect) and how much you really want the job.

If you're a guy, I would say a pair of khaki pants and a nice polo shirt (tucked in) would be appropriate. It wouldn't hurt to go one step further and try an ironed, button-down collared shirt with a tie. If you're a girl, it would be a great idea to wear dress pants or a knee-length skirt and a modest blouse. No flip-flops or gaudy jewelry!

Think of it this way: If you were trying to get someone's attention (maybe for a date), then you would fix yourself up nice, right? Well, in a job interview, you're trying to get the interviewer's attention. Now, go win that job!

WORKING

WHAT TYPE OF WORK IS BEST FOR SUMMER JOBS?

Answer

THINK OF WAYS YOU CAN BE SELF-EMPLOYED. You'll make a lot more per hour mowing grass, babysitting, pet sitting, detailing cars, cutting firewood and doing things like that than you'll ever make at a mall job or a fast-food job. By the time your employer takes taxes out, you almost wish you hadn't bothered.

You can make some serious money if you'll consider yourself a small-business owner. Just think about some ways you can make money off your skills and passions. Take a look around your neighborhood, your church and your community—what do people need and how can you provide it to them? It will be hard work, but making good money usually doesn't come easy. And at least this way you'll be your own boss and can set your own schedule.

Bottom line: Don't sit at home. Get creative about finding a good summer job. Before you know it, you'll be laying a foundation to win with money in the future.

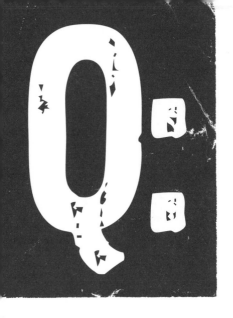

WHAT'S YOUR ADVICE FOR ASKING FOR A RAISE AT WORK?

It's always best to show how much you appreciate what you already have before you ask for more, so **START OFF BY TELLING YOUR BOSS HOW GRATEFUL YOU ARE FOR YOUR JOB**. Let him know how much you like working there, how much you've learned, and how much you appreciate the way he runs his business.

Next, detail some specific things about yourself that make you valuable to the company. Have you volunteered to work overtime? Did you take a class to learn a new skill that the company can benefit from? Have you suggested changes that saved the company time or money? Then ask your boss to reconsider your compensation based on those factors.

You can also provide a compensation study showing how your current pay compares to the salaries of people in the same line of work in comparably sized companies in your region. Your research will not only impress your boss, but it will prove that what you're asking for is fair.

Keep a pleasant attitude and smile a lot. Avoid any hint of bitterness or anger and never accuse your boss of paying you less than you think you're worth. You're trying to get him to see things your way, so don't put him on the defensive.

And remember, no matter how convincing your reasons are, the answer could still be no. Be prepared to accept that with the same professionalism you used to make the request.

> **"THERE IS MORE SATISFACTION IN RATIONAL SAVING THAN IN IRRATIONAL SPENDING."**
> — P. T. BARNUM

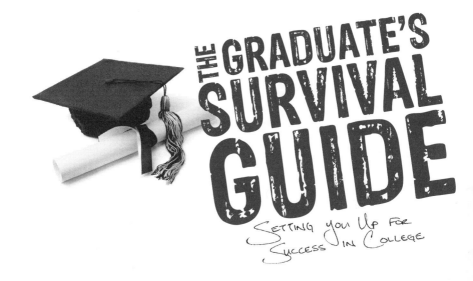

THE GRADUATE'S
SURVIVAL
GUIDE

Setting you Up for
Success in College

I'VE NEVER BEEN TAUGHT HOW TO SAVE, AND IT'S JUST REALLY HARD FOR ME TO DO. I REALLY LIKE TO SHOP. WHAT ARE SOME TIPS THAT WORK?

Answer

WE AREN'T BORN KNOWING HOW TO SAVE. IT'S A LEARNED SKILL. So for those of us who are spenders by nature, saving can be tough to learn. We really have to work hard at it.

Two things will help you: First, set some goals. What is it that you want to buy? What is something you need to save for, or how much money do you want to save? Set that as a goal, and then go for it.

Second, start looking at the math of investing. The earlier you start, the better. If you can start investing $100 a month from age 20 to 60, then that will add up to more than $1.1 million in a 12% mutual fund.

Save money slow and steady and you can become a millionaire.

I WANT TO BUY A NEW TV FOR MY DORM ROOM, AND I HAVE THE CASH FOR IT. IS IT OKAY TO BUY EXPENSIVE STUFF WHILE I AM STILL IN SCHOOL?

ANSWER

THE BIG QUESTION IS—DO YOU HAVE THE MONEY TO FINISH SCHOOL?
If you've got enough money saved to finish school, then buying some stuff is okay.

But keep this in mind: The best investment you will ever make is in yourself, not in a big-screen. A big-screen will not change your life, but an education will.

Before you start buying big toys, make sure that you've got tuition covered. Of course, that means textbooks and room and board too. Then you need some money in the bank for emergencies. We recommend three to six months of your expenses saved up in an emergency fund. If you've got all that taken care of, and if you're meeting all your monthly bills with no problem, then a giant TV won't make or break you.

SHOULD I HAVE TWO SAVINGS ACCOUNTS: ONE FOR NEXT SEMESTER'S TUITION AND ONE FOR EMERGENCIES?

YES. YOU SHOULD ALWAYS HAVE TWO BANK ACCOUNTS. Make sure you have an emergency fund that is only used for emergencies. And then you have your other savings account that can be used for other savings items.

Tuition would be a really good example of something that would go into this other account. If you're also saving up to buy new tires or something similar to that, you can put that in the same account with the tuition.

But keep your emergency fund separate. Keeping it separated will give you a mental reminder when you go to use your emergency savings for something that's not an emergency. You'll be reminded that buying a new couch is probably not an emergency, so you won't invade that space.

SAVING

I'M A FRESHMAN IN COLLEGE, AND I'M ALREADY THINKING I WANT TO GO TO LAW SCHOOL. HOW CAN I SAVE UP FOR THAT?

Answer

YOU HAVE PLENTY OF TIME, BUT START DOING RESEARCH NOW—for scholarships, grants and what type of school you want to attend. Apply for as many scholarships as you can. There's a ton of scholarship money out there, and millions of dollars of it go unclaimed every year. Consider this your part-time job.

Then, search online for a government agency that may be willing to pay for your law school if you agree to work for them for a few years after you graduate. It's kind of an indentured servitude deal, but that's a lot better than taking on $150,000 in debt!

Law school is expensive. So even if you receive a lot of scholarship money, you may still need more cash to pay for that degree. Work part time during the school year and full time during your summer breaks, and save as much as you can. You have plenty of time to make this work!

SAVING

HOW CAN I GET THE MOST
MONEY FOR THE ITEMS I SELL?
I DON'T WANT TO GET RIPPED
OFF, AND I'M NOT SURE HOW TO
GO ABOUT THIS WISELY. DO YOU
HAVE ANY TIPS?

ANSWER

FIRST, DON'T PLAY ALL YOUR CARDS FACEUP. The buyer will see that you really need the money.

Make sure you show the buyer that, if you don't get the amount you want, you fully intend to keep the item. That will show them that you only intend to deal with serious offers. It puts you back in the position of power, kind of like when you use walkaway power when buying something.

If you're selling antiques or collectible items, then get them appraised and sell them slightly below the appraised price. Showing the buyer that you are selling for less than the appraisal will make him feel like he is getting a deal while giving you the upper hand because you were armed with information.

Try out these tips and, like everything else, you will get better the more you practice. Have fun.

SAVING

"I NEVER WOULD HAVE BEEN ABLE TO TITHE THE FIRST MILLION DOLLARS I EVER MADE IF I HAD NOT TITHED MY FIRST SALARY, WHICH WAS $1.50 PER WEEK."
— JOHN D. ROCKEFELLER

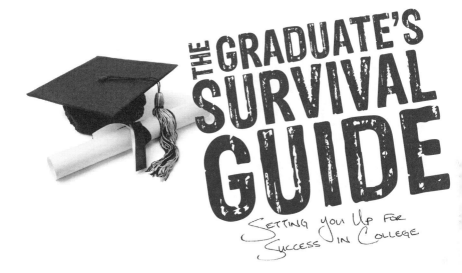

THE GRADUATE'S SURVIVAL GUIDE

Setting you Up for Success in College

GIVING

Q:

I UNDERSTAND THAT I NEED TO SAVE MONEY FOR NEXT SEMESTER'S TUITION AND MY EMERGENCY FUND. BUT IF I'M TRYING TO SAVE MONEY, SHOULD I WORRY ABOUT GIVING SOME OF IT AWAY?

Answer

That's a really good question. Rabbi Daniel Lapin reminds us that **ALMOST ALL OF OUR OPPORTUNITIES IN LIFE COME THROUGH PEOPLE.** In other words, you will get your raises, jobs, promotions and sales because of other people. And guess who people respond well to? Other people who are good, generous, spirited and giving.

Think about it. If you were the boss and you had a jerk and a good person working for you, who would you promote? Easy answer. You promote the good person every time. Who do you think professors like to help? Smart people? No. They do help smart people. But they like to help people who smile, engage them, look them in the eye, shake their hand with a firm handshake, introduce themselves, and are just all-around friendly people.

When you give, you're more likable, and givers have a tendency to win. Some of the most giving people in the world are millionaires and multimillionaires. There really is a direct correlation.

GIVING

I'M PRETTY STRAPPED FOR CASH RIGHT NOW, BUT I STILL WANT TO FIND A WAY TO GIVE. HOW MUCH MONEY SHOULD I GIVE FROM EACH PAYCHECK? AND, IF I CAN'T GIVE MONEY, HOW MUCH TIME SHOULD I VOLUNTEER?

Answer

START BY TAKING CARE OF YOURSELF—THE BASICS. After that, help others as much as you can.

The Jewish people have a wonderful tradition called the Havdalah service. In this service, a cup of wine is set into a saucer. They pour wine into the cup until it overflows into the saucer beneath. The point is that you are to take care of your own home and your own needs first. That's your cup. But as you continue to work and earn money, your overflow symbolizes what you can give to others.

As a college student, right now your first responsibility is to attend class, get good grades, and learn. Once you've taken care of your school needs, then you should definitely think of ways you can help out in your community. Work at a homeless shelter. Volunteer at a soup kitchen. Tithe to your church. Donate to charity.

Always make your budget work first—then give out of the overflow. If you're not afraid to work and balance taking care of yourself and others, then you'll have the character to become very wealthy and very generous.

GIVING

"YOU WILL QUICKLY FIND THAT THE GREATEST RATE OF RETURN YOU WILL EARN IS ON YOUR OWN PERSONAL SPENDING. BEING A SMART SHOPPER IS THE FIRST STEP TO GETTING RICH."

— MARK CUBAN

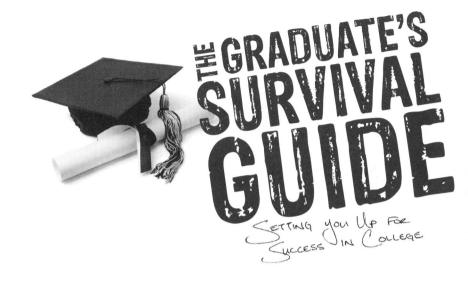

THE GRADUATE'S SURVIVAL GUIDE

Setting you Up For Success in College

BUYING A CAR

I'M ABOUT TO HEAD OFF TO COLLEGE, AND I WANT MY OWN CAR. WHAT ARE MY OPTIONS?

FIRST, YOU COULD WORK HARD AND SAVE MONEY TO BUY A NICE, USED CAR. If your parents are struggling financially, this may be your only option. You don't want your mom and dad taking out a car loan if they are already in debt. Not a good idea.

Work for a few months over the summer and save up a few thousand dollars to buy something that will get you around.

Now, you're probably wondering how you could save up that type of money on a part-time salary. First off, unless you're going to summer school, you've got the time to take a full-time job, so why not do that and save even more money? Skip the video games and make some cash!

If a part-time job is all you can manage during the school year, you can still save enough to pay cash for a car. Play with the numbers a little, and you'll discover that if you earn just $8 an hour and work 10 hours a week for two years, you'll have $6,000 to put toward a nice, used car.

A quick online search for used cars will show you plenty of great cars you can buy for $6,000 or less. You don't have to drive a beater, but, if you want something more than a $1,000 junker, you need to earn that money and pay cash.

Q:

I'VE NEVER BOUGHT A USED CAR BECAUSE MY PARENTS ALWAYS LEASE NEW CARS. WHAT DO I LOOK FOR IN A GOOD USED CAR?

Great question. **TAKE IT TO A GOOD MECHANIC AND PAY A SMALL FEE TO HAVE THEM DO AN INSPECTION ON THE CAR.** They can tell you everything that's right or everything that's wrong with it. Make sure they also do an analysis on the oil.

Sure, you want to look cool, but your primary goal should be to get a quality car that will get you where you need to go. A lot of people get a cool ride that might look good on the outside, but it's a piece of trash where it counts. If your car has a great paint job and a crummy engine, at least you'll look cool waiting for the tow truck on the side of the road.

Do your research. Look up the car's value on Kelley Blue Book, Edmunds or Yahoo! and see what it is selling for. Become an expert on the brand, make, model and year of that car. That way, when you go to buy, you don't get ripped off.

But here's the deal: Broke people care about what others think about their car. Rich people don't care. So you need to decide which one you are going to be—broke or rich?

And, don't forget, always pay cash!

BUYING
A CAR

Q:

I'VE BEEN DRIVING AN OLD, USED CAR FOR A WHILE NOW. I'M THINKING ABOUT GETTING A NEW ONE, AND I'VE MANAGED TO SAVE UP ABOUT $30,000 FROM MY JOBS. BUT EVERY TIME I GO TO A CAR DEALER, THEY WANT ME TO FINANCE A NEW CAR INSTEAD OF PAYING CASH FOR ONE. WHAT SHOULD I DO?

Answer

WHO CARES WHAT THE CAR DEALER WANTS? This is your purchase, not theirs! The dark secret of car lots is that car dealers make more money selling financing than they do selling cars. They always want you to take the loan because their commission is a lot better on financed cars.

But there's a bigger issue here. You have been industrious enough to scrape up $30,000 over the last few years. The worst thing you could do with that money is put it all into something that's going to go down in value like a rock.

New cars lose up to 70% of their value in the first four years. So if you buy a new $28,000 car as a freshman, it will be worth around $8,500 when you graduate—and that's true even if you finish in four years! Are you rich enough to throw $20,000 out the window while you're in college? Probably not. You don't need a brand-new car!

Once you've got a million dollars in the bank, then you can go out and buy a brand-new car. For now, you need to stick with good, used, low-mileage vehicles that are about three or four years old. And no, you won't be "buying someone else's problems" as long as you shop around and buy it right. You'll just be letting someone else take the hit on depreciation.

Think about finding and paying cash for a cool $10,000 car. You can get a great automobile for that kind of money, plus you'll still have most of your savings sitting there for emergencies or future purchases!

WHAT'S THE DIFFERENCE BETWEEN COLLISION AND LIABILITY CAR INSURANCE?

Answer

SHORT ANSWER: COLLISION TAKES CARE OF YOU; LIABILITY TAKES CARE OF THE OTHER GUY.

Collision insurance will replace your car if it ever gets totaled. Maybe you've had a friend who totaled his car but then got a new one from the insurance company. That's because he had collision coverage.

Comprehensive insurance is kind of like collision, but it covers damage to your car from something other than a wreck. Comprehensive steps in and takes care of you if your car is stolen, vandalized, damaged in a fire, blown away by a tornado, etc.

Liability insurance is when you tear up someone else's stuff. If you get in a wreck and someone in your car gets hurt, liability will cover that. If you tear up a neighbor's yard, break down their wall, or smash their car, liability will pay for that.

Liability insurance is a must; in fact, it's illegal to drive in most states without it! It's one of the best buys in insurance. Always get a lot of liability insurance—at least $500,000 worth. It practically costs pennies, but it could save hundreds of thousands of dollars in the long run!

BUYING A CAR

"HAVING IT ALL DOESN'T NECESSARILY MEAN HAVING IT ALL AT ONCE."

— STEPHANIE LUETKEHANS

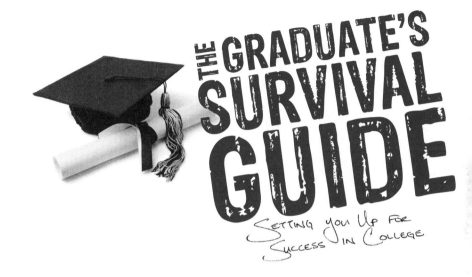

THE GRADUATE'S SURVIVAL GUIDE

Setting you Up For Success In College

I GOT A JOB RIGHT OUT OF HIGH SCHOOL EARNING $25,000 A YEAR. I ONLY HAVE AN $8,000 CAR LOAN, AND I'M THINKING ABOUT BUYING A HOME. IS NOW THE TIME TO BUY?

Congratulations on the job! **I KNOW IT'S TEMPTING TO SPEND YOUR NEW INCOME ON A HOME RIGHT AWAY, BUT YOU'RE JUST NOT READY YET.** You should buy a home only when you're debt-free, have an emergency fund of three to six months of expenses, and have a big down payment saved up. So your focus right now should be to pay off your car loan and start piling up cash!

You're also at a time of life where big changes are possible. You might decide you want to go to school or move to take a better job. A house and mortgage will limit your options.

So for now, plan to rent, get out of debt, and save, save, save! When the time comes to buy a home, you'll be in a much better financial position.

I'M ABOUT TO GRADUATE, AND TWO FRIENDS AND I ARE THINKING ABOUT BUYING A HOUSE TOGETHER. SHOULD WE DO IT? WE HAVE A LOT OF QUESTIONS.

ABSOLUTELY NOT. THAT'S NOT A GOOD IDEA AT ALL. Do this and you can almost guarantee that the three of you won't be talking to each other in a few years. You don't want to create a partnership. If you really want a house, then one of you should buy it and the other two should rent from the buyer.

Here's what will happen if you all buy the house together: One of you will get married, one of you will get mad about something and run off, and one of you will be left holding the bag—and all of you will get foreclosed on.

Don't do this deal.

WHAT'S THE DIFFERENCE BETWEEN AN ARM, A BALLOON MORTGAGE AND A FIXED MORTGAGE?

Answer

AN ARM IS AN ADJUSTABLE RATE MORTGAGE. YOU NEVER WANT TO TAKE OUT AN ARM. Why? Because the interest rate adjusts after a certain period of time, typically three to five years. This changes your payment every month. Your life has too many variables to mess with an ARM.

A balloon mortgage is another awful option. What happens here is that you pay the mortgage like it's a 30-year mortgage over the course of several years. And then all of a sudden, the entire balance on the mortgage comes due. So you're cruising along and you lose your job or you take some type of financial hit, and that's about the time your balloon payment is due.

A 15-year fixed-rate mortgage is the only thing you need to mess with. Make sure your payment is no more than one-fourth of your take-home pay. A fixed-rate is just that—fixed. It doesn't move up or down. It's predictable. Your interest rate never changes.

Of course, the best option of all is what we call the "100% Down Plan." That is, you pay cash for a house. Don't laugh this off too quickly. Start early enough and you could be living in a paid-for home by the time you're 30. If you work hard and make that happen, you'll be set for life.

BUYING A HOUSE

"THE BEST WAY TO GET RICH QUICK IS TO GET RICH SLOW. WHEN IT COMES TO WEALTH BUILDING, PERSEVERANCE WINS. SPRINTERS DO NOT. TRUE WEALTH BUILDING IS HARD AND TAKES TIME."

— DAVE RAMSEY

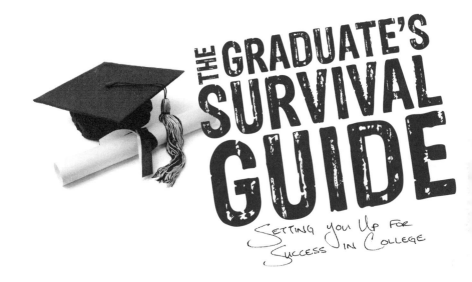

THE GRADUATE'S SURVIVAL GUIDE

Setting you up for Success in College

I'M A 21-YEAR-OLD COLLEGE STUDENT. I'VE GOT $1,000 IN THE BANK FOR MY EMERGENCY FUND, PLUS I'LL BE DEBT-FREE IN ABOUT SIX MONTHS. IS IT TOO EARLY TO BEGIN SAVING FOR RETIREMENT?

You could start a retirement fund, but **YOU MAY WANT TO START A "GRADUATION FUND" ON TOP OF YOUR EMERGENCY FUND.**

You're going to experience a lot of transition in the years after college, with new jobs, new locations and new relationships. All these things are going to require cash, because you don't want to start your new life by going back into debt.

Since you've still got some debt, just stick to the Baby Steps for now. You've already got your $1,000 emergency fund (Baby Step 1). Next, you'll knock out all your debts using the debt snowball, paying them off from smallest to largest (Baby Step 2). Then, Baby Step 3 is a fully funded emergency fund of three to six months of expenses, plus a little extra for the "transition expenses" after college. Once you're out of school, working, and you've got all this in place, you'll be ready for Baby Step 4, which is investing 15% of your income into retirement accounts like a Roth IRA or a company 401(k).

The best part of all this is that you're already thinking about this stuff before you get out of school. At 21, you're already on track for a fantastic start in life and you can look forward to being wealthy when you retire!

WHY SHOULD I START SAVING MONEY FOR RETIREMENT SO EARLY? DON'T I HAVE PLENTY OF TIME TO WORRY ABOUT THAT LATER?

WE HAVE TWO WORDS FOR YOU: COMPOUND INTEREST. This is a millionaire's best friend. It's really free money. Seriously. But don't take our word for it. Just check out this story of Ben and Arthur to understand the power of compound interest.

Ben is a pretty smart guy. At age 19, he started investing $2,000 a year into good mutual funds that averaged a 12% rate of return. After eight years of saving, Ben, then age 26, stopped putting money into his investments. So he put a total of ***$16,000*** into his investment funds.

Ben's brother, Arthur, took life a little easier during his college years and never thought about saving money. When he got his first "real" job at age 27, Arthur started putting $2,000 into mutual funds every year, and he kept doing this year after year his whole working life— until he turned 65. He got the same 12% rate of return as Ben, but ***he invested for 31 more years*** than Ben did. So Arthur invested a total of ***$78,000*** over 39 years.

When the brothers turned 65, they decided to compare their investment accounts. Who do you think had more? Ben, with his total of $16,000 invested over eight years, or Arthur, who invested $78,000 over 39 years?

Believe it or not, Ben came out ahead ... ***$700,000*** ahead! Arthur had a total of $1,532,166, while Ben was sitting on $2,288,996!

How did he do it? Starting early is the key. He put in less money but started eight years earlier. That's compound interest for you! It is a mathematical explosion that turned $16,000 into almost $2.3 million!

So what does this mean? The earlier you can start investing the better. Use the power of compound interest to your advantage.

THE EARLIER YOU CAN START INVESTING THE BETTER.

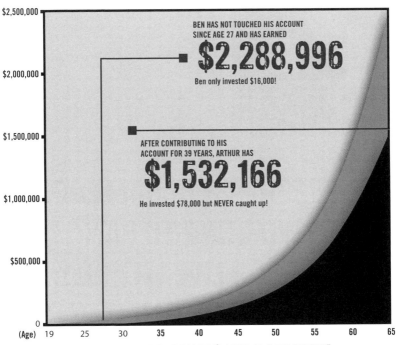

BEN HAS NOT TOUCHED HIS ACCOUNT
SINCE AGE 27 AND HAS EARNED

$2,288,996

Ben only invested $16,000!

AFTER CONTRIBUTING TO HIS
ACCOUNT FOR 39 YEARS, ARTHUR HAS

$1,532,166

He invested $78,000 but NEVER caught up!

SAVING ONLY $167 A MONTH!

I'M A FRESHMAN IN COLLEGE, AND I'M WORKING TO PAY FOR SCHOOL. I LIVE WITH MY PARENTS AND MY CAR IS PAID FOR, SO I DON'T HAVE ANY EXPENSES OTHER THAN TUITION. SHOULD I START SAVING FOR A HOUSE AND RETIREMENT NOW?

GREAT JOB! YOU'RE ALREADY LIGHT-YEARS BEYOND WHAT MOST OF YOUR CLASSMATES ARE DOING. Let's break this down into a few clear goals.

Your first goal is to save enough money to pay for your next semester of school with cash. Then, it's a good idea to save up an emergency fund of three to six months of your expenses. After that, you can start saving for things you're planning to do a few years from now, like buying a home or getting married.

If you still have some money to set aside, you can start investing with a Roth IRA. Invest in growth stock mutual funds with a history of good returns. You can invest up to $5,000 a year in a Roth IRA. A good financial advisor will set up the Roth IRA for you and help you choose your mutual funds.

If you take these steps while you're in school, you'll be in a great financial position when you graduate. And, you'll be on your way to becoming extremely wealthy when you're a little older.

RETIREMENT

Q:

MY PARENTS ARE STARTING TO TALK ABOUT RETIRING SOON. THAT GOT ME THINKING, "HOW MUCH DO I NEED TO RETIRE?"

Answer

IF YOU'RE ASKING QUESTIONS LIKE THAT IN COLLEGE, YOU'RE GOING TO BE RICH ONE DAY. That's awesome. You're going to retire with dignity because you're thinking about it.

The basic rule of thumb is that you need enough in your retirement accounts to be able to peel off 8% of it every year as your retirement income. So, if you want to live on $80,000 a year in retirement, you need $1 million in your account. That is, 8% of $1 million is $80,000. Get it?

What's so special about 8%? The lifetime stock market average is around 12%, so you can reasonably expect that as a lifetime average for your investments. Inflation is around 4%. So if your nest egg is earning 12%, you take out 8% to live on, and inflation eats 4%, that means you can live comfortably only on the interest and never touch the principal. Your $1 million will stay put and you'll just live off the income your investment makes in interest.

If you do that you'll retire with dignity. In fact, you'll be in the top 5% of Americans. That's all there is to it. Keep on looking to the future with this type of vision, and you will definitely succeed in life.

I'M STARTING COLLEGE IN THE FALL, BUT NEXT MONTH I'LL RECEIVE AN INHERITANCE OF ABOUT $40,000. I DON'T KNOW ANYTHING ABOUT STOCKS, MUTUAL FUNDS OR CDS, BUT I DON'T WANT TO LOSE ALL THIS MONEY. I DON'T HAVE ANY DEBT, SO WHAT SHOULD I DO?

Answer

It's great that you're asking questions. **ONE OF THE FASTEST WAYS TO LOSE MONEY IS TO INVEST IT WHEN YOU DON'T KNOW HOW INVESTING WORKS.**

For now, a simple savings account is fine. Park $30,000 in there and just forget about it for a while. Then use $5,000 to set up an emergency fund, and blow $5,000 on some things just for you. After all, spending and having fun with money is one of the things it's good for!

Get with a quality financial advisor and start learning about your options. Whatever you do, do not let someone else tell you how to invest your money. Your advisor's job is to teach you how this stuff works so that you can make your *own* decisions. If you're talking to someone who just wants to tell you what to do, then cut him or her loose and find someone with the heart of a teacher who can really help you learn this stuff.

Once you've educated yourself on investing, you'll see that if you put that remaining $30,000 into good growth stock mutual funds, by the time you're ready to retire you'll be looking at *millions*.

Talk about being able to retire with dignity and change your family tree!

RETIREMENT

WHAT ARE THE COMMON TRAITS OF A MILLIONAIRE?

Answer

There's a great book out by Tom Stanley called *The Millionaire Next Door*. It's the most well-researched study ever completed of a group of millionaires.

First, they usually buy and drive used cars. A lot of them are self-employed. Most of them are first-generation rich, meaning they didn't start with Daddy's money. So that says a lot. **YOU DON'T HAVE TO START WITH A LOT TO END UP WITH A LOT.**

Another one of the key qualities you'll find with the typical millionaire is that they really have no need to impress other people. Broke people try to impress others. Rich people don't care what other people think.

So you need to actually have a plan in which you don't care what the broke people think. If you've got that state of mind, then you are on your way to being a millionaire.

Finally, don't try to get rich quick. The best way to build wealth is to get rich slow. Get-rich-quick schemes never work. The tortoise beats the hare every time they run the race. Do smart things over and over, and do that over a long period of time, and you'll win the race.

MORE RESOURCES

Visit **daveramsey.com** for more information and resources to help you learn how to manage money and avoid debt.

For more information on scheduling **RACHEL CRUZE** or any of our speakers for your next event, visit **daveramsey.com/speakers** or call **888.284.2488.**

Follow Rachel on Twitter at **@rachelcruze**

SAMPLE RESUME

John Q. Public

402111 Little Drive
Lamponia, TN 13579
johnp@example.com
555-123-4567

OBJECTIVE
To obtain a position working as a camp counselor.

EDUCATION

Completed three years of college prep coursework at Washington High School.
Projected graduation date: May 2009 GPA: 3.0

WORK EXPERIENCE

Junior Reserve Officer Training Corps, Lamponia High School (2007-present)
  ➢ Rank: Sergeant First Class
Jeffrey's Grille, Lamponia (2006-present)
  ➢ Salad prep and fry cook
  ➢ Bus boy and dishwasher

VOLUNTEER POSITIONS

Crew Leader, YMCA Summer Camp (2004-2008)
  ➢ Guided children in various activities
  ➢ Assisted children with creative projects
Coaching Assistant, Lamponia Middle School Wrestling Program (2006-2008)
  ➢ Coached athletes in the sport of wrestling
  ➢ Educated athletes about wrestling
  ➢ Prepared facilities for tournaments
Coaching Assistant, Thompson County Wrestling Club (2006-2008)
Program Volunteer, Lamponia Community Church, Homeless Ministry (2005-2008)
  ➢ Enlisted homeless men in games, activities, and conversation

EXTRACURRICULAR ACTIVITIES

Wrestling Team, Lamponia Middle School
Junior Varsity Wrestling Team, Lamponia High School, 2005-present
  ➢ Iron Man Award
Wrestling Clubs
  ➢ Thompson County Wrestling Club
  ➢ Hopeville Jr. Wrestling Club
  ➢ Lamponia Wrestling Club

HOW TO MAKE A BUDGET

"A budget is telling your money where to go instead of wondering where it went." —John C. Maxwell

There's nothing scary about budgeting—it's simply addition and subtraction!

Use the budgeting form on page 129 as a starting point and add or remove items based on your needs. Start by writing down how much you earn each month on the "Income" line at the top.

Next, list everything you spend money on each month. A great place to start is charitable giving. Deciding how much to give each month will give you perspective as you work through the rest of the budget.

Now allocate some of your money for your saving goals like a new phone, a new car or even retirement.

Finally, tally up your bills and expenses that fall into the "Housing," "Utilities," "Food," "Transportation" and "Personal" categories. Organize them so they make sense to you, and don't leave anything out.

Total all your line items to determine your total monthly necessities, then subtract your total monthly necessities from your monthly income. If the sum is zero, congratulations! You've given every dollar a name! If you have money left over, you can add it to your budget for saving or giving. A negative number means you need to reduce some of your budget items so that you're living within your means.

Budgeting takes practice, so yours won't be perfect the first time. Keep at it, and you'll see that you can achieve your goals and have more than enough for everything you want to do—if you plan your money on paper before the month begins. Now get started!

BASIC STUDENT BUDGET

MONTHLY INCOME: $_____

EXPENSE ITEMS	MONTHLY TOTAL	RECOMMENDED %
GIVING	_____	10-15%
SAVING		5-10%
General Savings	_____	
Emergency Fund	_____	
Next Semester: Tuition, Books, Fees	_____	
HOUSING		25-35%
Rent / Rental Insurance	_____	
UTILITIES		5-10%
Cell Phone	_____	
Electric	_____	
Cable / Internet	_____	
Water / Trash	_____	
FOOD		5-15%
Groceries / Meal Plan	_____	
Eating Out	_____	
TRANSPORTATION		10-15%
Car Payment	_____	
Gas / Oil Change / Repairs & Tires	_____	
Registration & Insurance	_____	
Public Transportation	_____	
Trips & Traveling	_____	
PERSONAL		5-10%
Clothing / Laundry	_____	
Personal Hygiene / Toiletries	_____	
Entertainment	_____	
Blow Money	_____	
Health / Medical	_____	
OTHER MISC.	_____	5-10%

TOTAL EXPENSES: $_____

$_____ - $_____ = $_____

(Monthly Income)   (Total Expenses)   (This number should be zero.)

BALANCING YOUR ACCOUNT

The idea of balancing your account may seem tedious and unnecessary, but it's actually easy—and worth it! You can track your spending, avoid bounced checks, and catch mistakes the bank makes. Plus, you'll always know your actual balance. Remember, when you take responsibility for your money, you'll have more of it!

HERE'S HOW YOU DO IT

You can use a checkbook register, spreadsheets or online forms. Whatever the format, make sure you include the date of the transaction, where you spent the money, and the amount. You will also need three other columns: Debit, Credit and Balance.

First, record every transaction you make through your checking account, including checks, debit card purchases and deposits. Keep receipts of every transaction to make sure you don't forget to record an item. Then, list any amounts spent under the "Debit" column. When you make deposits, list them under the "Credit" column. Finally, after each transaction—debit or credit—calculate your balance by **subtracting debits** or **adding credits** to your previous balance. See the example on page 131.

Balancing your account takes a little bit of work, but it will save you the headaches and fees that come with money mistakes. See pages 22–23 for more reasons why you should balance your account.

SAMPLE ACCOUNT REGISTER

Check Register

✓	Check #	Date	Transaction Description	Payment (-)	Deposit (+)	Balance
	5671	8/12	One Stop Grocery	57.40		507.06
	5672	8/14	Electric Company	101.00		406.06
		8/14	Paycheck		700.00	1106.06
	5673	8/16	Telephone Company	50.00		1056.06
	5674	8/19	One Stop Grocery	66.00		990.06
		8/16	Bank Service Charge	2.50		$987.56

NOTES